nas felicità 幸福 laime ಸಂತ beatitudo 행복 среќа laime ke

intentizza lykke شادی szczęście felicidade счастье срећа

astie felicidad furaha sreča lycka மகிழ்ச்சி mutluluk щастя e

anh phúc ความสุข hapusrwydd happiness felicidade le bonh

appiness счастье geluk щастя lumturi سعادة шчасце երջանկ

oşbəxtlik zoriontasuna सुख felicitat щастие 幸福 sreća geluk

ěstí kaligayahan onni felicidade le bonheur ბედნიერება glü

τυχία सुख kontantman שמחה सुख boldogság hamingja kebah

nas felicità 幸福 laime ಸಂತ beatitudo 행복 среќа laimė ke

intentizza lykke شادی szczęście felicidade счастье срећа

astie felicidad furaha sreča lycka மகிழ்ச்சி mutluluk щастя e

anh phúc ความสุข hapusrwydd happiness felicidade le bonh

appiness счастье geluk щастя lumturi سعادة шчасце երջանկ

oşbəxtlik zoriontasuna सुख felicitat щастие 幸福 sreća

ěstí kaligayahan onni felicidade le bonheur ბედნიერება glü

τυχία सुख kontantman שמחה सुख boldogság hamingja kebah

nas felicità 幸福 laime ಸಂತ beatitudo 행복 среќа laimė ke

intentizza lykke شادی szczęście felicidade счастье срећа

astie felicidad furaha ಆನಂದಮು sreča lycka மகிழ்ச்சி mutluluk

anh phúc ความสุข hapusrwydd happiness felicidade le bonh

appiness счастье geluk щастя lumturi سعادة шчасце երջանկ

oşbəxtlik zoriontasuna सुख felicitat щастие 幸福 sreća geluk

ěstí kaligayahan onni ευτυχία felicidade le bonheur ბედნიერ

τυχία सुख kontantman שמחה सुख boldogság hamingja kebah

nas felicità 幸福 laime ಸಂತ beatitudo 행복 среќа laimė ke

intentizza lykke شادی szczęście felicidade счастье срећа

astie felicidad furaha sreča lycka மகிழ்ச்சி mutluluk щастя e

anh phúc ความสุข hapusrwydd happiness felicidade le bonh

appiness счастье geluk щастя lumturi سعادة шчасце երջանկ

oşbəxtlik zoriontasuna सुख felicitat щастие 幸福 sreća geluk

ěstí kaligayahan onni felicidade le bonheur ბედნიერება glü

τυχία सुख kontantman שמחה सुख boldogság hamingja kebah

nas felicità 幸福 laime ಸಂತ beatitudo 행복 среќа laimė ke

intentizza lykke شادی szczęście felicidade счастье срећа

astie felicidad furaha sreča lycka மகிழ்ச்சி mutluluk щастя e

anh phúc ความสุข hapusrwydd happiness felicidade le bonh

There are more than seven billion minds on this planet, but only one heart.

True communication occurs through the heart.

True happiness is an open heart.

Published by Porpoise Press
www.porpoisepress.com

PORPOISE
PRESS

First published in the USA | **2012**

ISBN 978-0-9872323-0-4

SAY
HELLO TO
HAPPINESS

MICHAEL ADAMEDES

&

ROBERT MICHAEL PRIOR

Illustrations by
Tetiana Koldunenko

Layout by
Veacha Sen

This

book is dedicated
to our parents,
Adam and Helen Adamedes,
and Bob and Sonia Prior.
Thank you for bringing us into
this world and for all your love,
support and wisdom.

TABLE OF CONTENTS

■ ABOUT **MICHAEL ADAMEDES**

Michael has been a clinical psychotherapist in private practice since 1982. His inner journey has taken him from studies in Morocco under the enlightened master Ahmid Sufi, through two years with yogi Satyananda Saraswati, to more than twenty years practice in meditation. His philosophy encompasses a respect for a diverse range of beliefs and cultures.

He also understudied the pioneering rebirther Ahrara Carisbrooke and established Australia's first rebirthing clinic, Euroa Centre. He has practised in many countries, including Australia, England, Hong Kong, Indonesia, New Zealand, Russia and the United States and is the founder of Inner Peace Mastery, which has been conducting personal development seminars and retreats since 1987.

Michael is an astute detective of the unconscious mind. Within the first hour of counselling a client, he can usually identify their patterns of self-limiting thinking and the causes of their self-sabotaging behaviours. He has created and developed Dysfunctional Pattern Clearing ©, a therapy for releasing a person's negative psychological and emotional patterns.

Many of his clients have experienced a transformation from being alone and unhappy to falling in love and finding their soul mate, from never having a cent in the bank to being able to buy investment properties, or from being constantly depressed and disillusioned to being vital and happy.

Inspired by Sondra Ray and Leonard Orr's teachings on self-limiting beliefs, Michael sought to unify and simplify their work. In 2004, he came to the conclusion that any unhappiness or stress is the result of just three categories of primal self-limiting beliefs. His remarkable discovery is revealed to the general public for the first time in this book.

Michael explains the origins of this book, "For about six months I had been contemplating writing a book of affirmations. Then, in August 2008, while conducting a personal development retreat in Bali, I sat down at my laptop one evening and the skeleton of the book emerged effortlessly over the next three days. At times, during the writing process, I had tears of joy as the power of the words overcame me."

"I showed my draft to my friend and colleague, Robert Prior, who was so inspired by it that he offered to collaborate on the project. Together, we have developed it into a powerful yet simple tool that we hope will transform the lives of people across the world."

ABOUT **ROBERT PRIOR**

Robert is one of those rare people who is able to balance the left and right hemispheres of the brain. He is a brilliant and inspiring mathematics teacher, logical and thorough, while also being creative and fun. One of his greatest strengths is his ability to make complex matters seem simple.

His accomplishments include establishing PRIOR Education in 1976, Australia's leading tuition college for secondary school students, which has helped more than twenty thousand students gain entry into their chosen university courses.

Robert is also a musician and a member of the band People Like That. With Glenn Bidmead, he has composed and recorded 31 songs that bring to life the affirmations of the 31 day programme in this book. He has also promoted the Australian tours of a number of international musicians.

In late 1991, during a period of major emotional upheaval, Robert realised that his old ways of thinking weren't working any more. He turned to self-help books, self-examination, meditation and the guidance of inspirational people. According to Robert, "I made the startling discovery that, although it seemed that other people were the cause of my upsets, my emotions were actually being created by my own mind."

"For most of my life, I had been operating predominantly on logic and rationality. If I couldn't prove something or experience it directly, it didn't exist. However, because that approach was no longer making me happy, I made a commitment to finding a deep and lasting inner peace. So I started to adopt a whole new way of thinking about myself and life in general."

With this more enlightened outlook, Robert was able to help his students gain a greater sense of purpose and direction, which translated into a dramatic increase in their self-esteem and academic success.

During one particularly difficult period, Robert was referred to Michael Adamedes for some counselling. He found Michael's innovative techniques so effective that he quickly found that he no longer needed therapy. An interesting outcome was that Robert and Michael soon became good friends and started collaborating on various personal development projects.

"It has been an absolute thrill writing this book with Michael and we truly hope that it can help you to find a deep and lasting happiness and inner peace."

HELLO AND WELCOME!

We hope you enjoy reading this book as much as we enjoyed writing it.

Did you know that you are magnificent beyond all description?

Within you lies an infinite reservoir of love and prosperity. You are far greater, more loving and more spectacular than you can even begin to imagine.

Here we all are together on our tiny spherical rock, hurtling through space at one hundred thousand kilometres per hour, sharing this extraordinary journey, discovering who we are and why we are here. Life is a miracle and we are miraculous.

The truth is simple. We will share with you the simple truths about creating and sustaining a higher level of happiness in your life. We will show you how to dissolve your stress, strife and struggle, and awaken your inner state of love and happiness.

Your every act of love and compassion is a significant personal achievement. As you become more loving and accepting of others, judgement and criticism will disappear and your life will become a joyful experience of ease and flow.

Thank you for your special gift of love to our human family... and thank you for being your own unique self.

Wishing you peace, health and happiness.

Shine on!

Michael and Robert

Aren't babies and young children delightful?

They are naturally joyful and easily swept away by the wonderment of life.

Did you realise that any unhappiness or stress that you have experienced in your life has been learned?

Are you ready to learn how to tap into your natural state of happiness and joy?

SECTION 1

MASTERING
YOUR THOUGHTS
& FEELINGS

HISTORICAL
PERSPECTIVE

> " The key to our happiness lies within ourselves and can be tapped into by understanding our own psychological and emotional conditioning. "

Human history has seen the advent of the Agricultural, Industrial and Technological Revolutions. These major developments focused primarily on shaping our external world.

In the early twentieth century, the focus for human advancement turned inward in a quest to discover how the human mind works and how we create emotions and the circumstances of our lives.

Starting with Sigmund Freud, the father of modern psychology, and continuing with important thinkers such as Carl Jung, Abraham Maslow, Stanislav Grof and John Bradshaw, the Self-Awareness Revolution gained momentum.

One of the most important discoveries of these great thinkers was that, contrary to the popular belief that we are the helpless victims of our external circumstances, the key to our happiness lies within ourselves and can be tapped into by understanding our own psychological and emotional conditioning.

THE NATURE
OF HAPPINESS

> " *By changing your interpretation of life on a conscious and unconscious level, you will improve your entire experience of life.* "

Is it possible to be
happy all the time?

Happiness is actually your natural state. As we will explore later, any stress or unhappiness that you have ever experienced has been learned.

We will teach you to think in ways that will make you feel happier. As a result, you will find yourself remaining calm and centred in situations that used to upset you. Over time, you will experience feelings of happiness more often.

It is our belief that it is ultimately possible to be happy all the time.

Do you really
want to be happy?

Many people say that they want to be happy, but they are either not prepared to do what it takes to be happy or they don't believe it is actually possible for them.

It takes self-discipline and commitment to release the unhappiness you have learned and see the higher purpose in your daily life.

To be truly happy, you need to be honest with yourself and committed to letting go of what doesn't work for you. You also need to be willing to explore some radically new ways of thinking.

What is stopping you
from being happy now?

Some common responses to this question are:

- » "I don't have enough money."
- » "I don't like my job."
- » "I don't have a partner."
- » "I'm worried about my exams."
- » "I don't have my own home."
- » "The economy is in a mess."
- » "My mother and father are unhappy."
- » "My partner drives me crazy."
- » "My kids won't listen to me."

There is no doubt that these issues can create challenges in your life, but do you really believe that these external factors are the cause of your emotions?

For example, is it possible to be broke and still happy? Is it possible to be rich and unhappy? Most people would agree that these two scenarios are possible. So what is the underlying cause of your happiness or unhappiness?

What is the
key to happiness?

To feel better about yourself and your life, it is important to understand what creates your feelings. Many people believe that their feelings are created by the people and events in their lives. But in reality, it's how you interpret these events that creates your feelings. By changing your interpretation of life on a conscious and unconscious level, you will inevitably change your feelings – and ultimately improve your entire experience of life.

Happiness comes from within and is a direct result of the way that you choose to think about things. Being happy is a choice that only you can make. When you make a serious commitment to finding a deep and permanent state of happiness and inner peace, you will move towards achieving exactly that.

THOUGHTS FEELINGS & BELIEFS

> *The quality of your thoughts is the most important factor in determining your level of happiness, your day today circumstances and the quality of your entire life.*

What are **thoughts?**

You spend all day thinking about things. Some of your thoughts are purely practical, such as "What do I need at the supermarket?" or "What time does my meeting start this morning?". These types of thoughts are useful to you because they help you organise your life.

At other times, you may have worrying thoughts such as "How am I going to pay this pile of bills?", "Will she return my phone call?", "What does my future hold?" or "I'm getting older and it's starting to show".

A thought is simply an idea. You spend so much time thinking, but how often do you actually think about the process of thinking? For example, do you feel free to choose different thoughts? If so, what are your choices? What are the consequences of your various choices? Do your thoughts represent reality or merely a perspective you have chosen to adopt? Which types of thoughts lead to happiness? How can you make permanent, positive changes to the way you think?

The quality of your thoughts is the most important factor in determining your level of happiness, your day to-day circumstances and the quality of your entire life.

What are conscious and
unconscious thoughts?

To become a happy and successful person, it is important to appreciate the difference between your conscious and unconscious thoughts. Quite simply, your conscious thoughts are the ones you are aware of and your unconscious thoughts are those you are not aware of.

For example, imagine that you are at a party and you see an attractive person on the other side of the room. You make a conscious decision to introduce yourself and, while walking across the room, you notice that you are perspiring, feeling anxious and experiencing tension in your stomach. You then find yourself saying the most inane things! Why is this happening? It is because some of your unconscious thoughts have been activated - possibly a belief of being inadequate or a fear of being rejected.

What are
feelings?

Feelings are just physical sensations occurring in your body.

Reactive feelings can be placed into three categories:

① *Fear, from mild anxiety to absolute terror and sometimes paralysis*
② *Anger, from minor irritation to rage*
③ *Sadness, from mild disappointment to traumatic grief and depression*

Natural feelings can also be placed into three categories:

> ① **Love, which encompasses kindness, affection, gratitude, compassion and acceptance.**
> ② **Joy, which includes pleasure, happiness, elation and ecstasy.**
> ③ **Peace, which is the feeling of being calm, relaxed and centred.**

You can tell when you are at peace with yourself because you have a certainty that everything is okay and will be okay.

There is an important distinction between reactive and natural feeling states. Your reactive feelings (commonly referred to as your "emotions") arise from conditioned (that is, learned) responses in your conscious and unconscious mind, whereas your natural feelings are inherent to your true nature.

Thoughts, speech and actions arising when experiencing a reactive feeling are unreliable and often cause conflict, struggle and scarcity.

In contrast, when operating from your natural feelings, your decisions can be relied upon to create a life of ease, clarity and abundance.

Your journey to happiness involves detaching from your reactive feelings of fear, anger and sadness, which will thus allow you to experience your natural feelings of love, joy and peace.

What is the connection
between thoughts and feelings?

Imagine that you are driving in congested peak hour traffic. Your car is crawling along and you are running late for a meeting. If you think "I can't believe this - I'm running late - this is ridiculous", how would you feel?

Alternatively, if you choose to think, "There's nothing I can do about this, so I'll just accept it, relax and think about my upcoming meeting, or maybe I'll just enjoy the radio", how would that make you feel?

Clearly, if you choose the former thoughts, you would feel quite frustrated. However, if you have the wisdom to choose the latter thoughts, you would obviously feel calmer, even though the traffic situation is still out of your control.

So you can see that the way you choose to think about a situation can have a profound positive influence on your short-term feelings.

Does positive thinking work
with more intense feelings?

In the previous scenario about running late for a meeting, it should be fairly easy for you to change your feelings, simply by choosing more positive thoughts.

But does this approach work in more extreme situations, such as the death of a loved one, bankruptcy or betrayal by a spouse? Most people would be devastated by the occurrence of one of these events and may take years to recover.

Although choosing positive thoughts may not produce immediate relief with these more intense feelings, a sustained focus on positive thinking will always accelerate your return to emotional stability. You will also be moved to a higher state of awareness, with greater compassion, wisdom and peace of mind.

In fact, many psychologists believe that your choice of thoughts will ultimately determine your feelings about any situation.

What if positive thinking
still doesn't work?

Some people hold feelings of resentment and betrayal all their lives. They may be advised to let go of this resentment and even believe that it is a good idea to let it go, but they still find it hard to do. Sometimes the uncomfortable feelings just won't go away. Every time these people think of a particular person or situation they become resentful. Why is it so hard for them to let go of those unpleasant feelings and move on? To answer this question, you need to understand the way your mind and body create your thoughts and feelings.

The physiology of
thoughts and feelings

There is a fundamental difference between thoughts and feelings.

Thoughts are electrical. They are mainly electrical signals passing between the synapses of your brain and they act very quickly.

Feelings, however, are mostly chemical reactions, caused by substances called neuropeptides, taking place in the bloodstream and organs of your body. A chemical reaction occurs at a much slower rate than an electrical discharge - in fact, hundreds and sometimes thousands of times slower.

It takes the average person less than one second to change a thought and, on average, about five to ten minutes to change an emotion. That is, emotions operate hundreds of times slower than thoughts. Many people take years to let go of a deep hurt or disappointment, but with training, it is possible to change an emotion in a few seconds.

To experience positive feelings, you may need to think positively about a situation for up to ten minutes before the neuropeptides in your bloodstream actually take effect and you start to feel better. We will teach you the thoughts that most effectively accelerate this process.

Other ways of
creating positive feelings

1. With physical exercise, your body releases endorphins that change your body chemistry and naturally make you feel better.

2. Massage helps you to relax and relieves muscular tension.

3. Taking a hot bath increases your core body temperature and speeds up your metabolism, thereby enabling you to physically and emotionally detoxify. Caution must be taken if you suffer from a heart condition, are pregnant, have recently undergone surgery or have an open wound.

4 Aromatherapy and reiki help you to release stress and tension.

5 Dancing, playing a musical instrument, singing, whistling or listening to uplifting music all create positive feelings.

6 Painting, sculpting and pottery help many people release stress.

7 Being in touch with nature - walking in the park, strolling along a beach, going for a hike or seeing a sunrise or sunset - are all inspiring experiences.

8 Hatha yoga is a science of body movement that harmonises the mind, body and spirit. Other forms of yoga may also be helpful in calming the mind and releasing stress.

9 When faced with a stressful situation, taking several deep breaths and focusing your attention on your breath will instantly relax you.

10 Meditation is a powerful way to turn off your mind and transcend reactive feelings, such as fear, anger and grief. If you have the discipline, patience and commitment required, you will reap enormous benefits.

11 Laughter is said to be the best form of medicine. Watching a funny movie, having a laugh with friends or family and generally looking at the amusing side of life are all great ways to create positive feelings.

What is the difference
between a thought and a belief?

Consider Frank, who is a confident public speaker. He has a passion for sharing his knowledge of computing and does not feel nervous when addressing a group. Unconsciously, he holds the thought "I am a great speaker", which is accompanied by a positive feeling. Frank believes in his presenting skills.

In contrast, Frank's colleague Henry feels nervous when addressing a group. Although he says to himself, "I am a good presenter. I can do this easily", he still feels anxious. His positive thoughts have not yet become positive beliefs, because they are not accompanied by positive feelings. Henry does not truly believe in his presenting skills.

Thus, a thought is simply an idea, whereas a belief is an idea that you hold with an accompanying feeling.

THE
PERSONALITY

> **" A key to happiness is to consciously adopt a more benevolent, inclusive and secure view of life. "**

What is the
Personality?

In everyday conversation, when someone is easy to talk to and fun to be with, we may say, "She has a great personality". However, in this book we will use the term "Personality" to refer to the sum total of your beliefs, emotions and behaviours.

Your Personality includes the conscious and unconscious memories in your mind and body. It is the result of all of your experiences from conception onward, plus the ancestral and genetic qualities you inherited from your parents, grandparents and forebears.

Your Personality determines your unconscious, habitual ways of responding to situations. However, your habitual responses are often attempts to protect yourself from rejection, scarcity or danger and tend to create the opposite effect of what you intended, thus making you more unhappy.

A key to happiness is to become aware of when you are behaving from your reactive Personality and consciously choose to stop doing it by adopting a more benevolent, inclusive and secure view of life. Our aim is to guide you towards achieving this.

Who is responsible
for your Personality?

Jody drinks alcohol to excess. Who is to blame? Her father, who is an alcoholic? Her mother, who always wanted Jody to be a high achiever? Is it her boss's fault for giving her too much work and setting unreasonable deadlines? Is the government to blame for mismanaging the economy, creating a high level of unemployment and making it almost impossible for her to find alternative employment? Sometimes she blames herself for being too weak and afraid to change.

Blaming yourself, other people, the economy, the government or other factors doesn't help. The problem with this type of thinking is that nothing changes. All you succeed in doing is creating more justification for being unhappy.

From his clinical counselling experience since 1982, Michael has concluded that at least 90 percent of your Personality is inherited. Because your inheritance goes back many generations, neither you nor your parents are to blame for your weaknesses and shortcomings.

The Personality is a
self-induced hypnotic trance

A common trick that stage hypnotists use is to gather a number of people and hypnotise them into believing that the onion they are eating is an apple. Each person can see that the others are eating onions and is incredulous at this sight. However, each believes that they themselves are eating an apple!

This is an example of how the human mind is able to delude itself. Some people may say that the stage hypnotist was responsible for creating the delusion, but it was actually the participants who chose to give away part of their perception of reality. It is impossible to put an unwilling person into a trance.

This phenomenon extends to our everyday state of mind. Unintentionally, you are continually giving away part of your perception of reality, because you want reality to conform to your expectations. This started when you were a child and wanted to be loved by your parents, so you adopted their perspective of life as your perspective. In time, this perspective became your worldview, which you then believed to be reality.

For example, if your parents believed that money was scarce and work was a struggle, it is likely that you would now believe this to be true. Conversely, if they believed that money is plentiful and work is a joy, then you would probably have adopted that belief. In either case, your life's circumstances reflect your adopted perspective.

When we say that "the Personality is a self-induced hypnotic trance", we mean that you have hypnotised yourself into equating your beliefs with reality. No one else put you into your trance. Although you were brought up in the culture of your family, friends and others, you and you alone have convinced yourself that your beliefs represent reality.

We can often see limiting patterns of behaviour in other people, but it can be much more difficult to see them within ourselves. A key to accelerating your personal development is your willingness to accept the fact that you are blind to many aspects of your own conditioning.

Of course, you may have inherited or acquired many powerful and positive traits, which could include courage, integrity, determination, compassion and generosity. But you may also have acquired limiting beliefs of unworthiness, struggle, scarcity and so on.

You are usually not aware that your Personality is a trance state until the spell of the trance is broken by what is perceived to be an undesirable event. When this happens, it may feel uncomfortable and sometimes unfair.

A more useful perspective is that you have arrived at a fork in the road. One approach is to resist the change and avoid the discomfort, which may lead to blaming others and perhaps escaping through substance and/or process addiction.

The more enlightened path is to accept responsibility for the events in your life and view them as opportunities to break out of your trance and create a more abundant, joyful and loving life.

Can you change
your Personality?

Henry thinks, "I get nervous when I'm in front of a group and that's just human nature. That's my personality. I guess that's how I'll always be." If this were true, there would be no way of changing ourselves and improving our lives, other than waiting for an improvement in our external environment.

When training racehorses, a breeder has two variables to work with: genetics and environment. He will look at the sire and mare's bloodlines to determine the likelihood of creating a champion. Once he has a good breed, he must do his best with the environmental factors of diet, health and exercise. That's the best he can do.

Unlike horses or other animals, we have three variables that determine the quality of our lives: genetics, environment and introspection (our ability to examine our own mental and emotional processes). That is how we humans are able to rise above the perceived limitations of our genetics and environment.

For example, in the Olympic Games, numerous people through sheer courage and determination have risen above the perceived limitations of their backgrounds and become champions.

So, the good news is that you can change the aspects of your Personality that you are not happy with!

How can you change the
limiting aspects of your Personality?

There are three ways to change the limiting aspects of your Personality.

1. The most common way is through some kind of emotional breakdown such as the end of a relationship, going bankrupt or a life-threatening illness. This triggers a fundamental re-evaluation of values, goals and beliefs, which precipitates a shift in identity. Who am I? What's life about? What's really important? Many people say that this is when they started to grow up.

2. A second, less-frequent way to change the limiting aspects of your Personality is through what the Japanese call satori: a flash of sudden awareness or enlightenment that creates a fundamental shift in values, goals and beliefs.

3. The third way is through a sustained, focused effort over an extended period of time. This involves the systematic changing of limiting beliefs to more resourceful ones and letting go of emotional attachment to events.

In Section 2, we will teach you the third way and show you how to master your thinking and feelings through the use of mental scripts, commonly known as affirmations. These affirmations have been designed to neutralise the three primal self-limiting beliefs of the unconscious mind, which are explained in detail in Section 3.

EMOTIONAL
RESPONSIBILITY

> " *Emotional responsibility is the ability to remain detached, open and accepting of yourself, others and life's circumstances at all times.* "

You are 100 percent responsible for creating your own happiness and the best way to achieve this is by adopting Emotional Responsibility.

Emotional Responsibility is the ability to take charge of your emotions by remaining detached, open and accepting of yourself, others and life's circumstances at all times.

A golden opportunity to take charge of your emotions is when you are feeling very angry, hurt or afraid. However, this is the time when many people feel most justified in blaming themselves or others. They remain upset and thus lose the opportunity to learn to take responsibility for their emotions.

Remaining upset is an unhelpful habit, which is often perpetuated by:

1. *A sense of injustice, arising from a feeling of being treated unfairly,*

2. *A desire to punish by thoughts, speech or actions, or*

3. *Not having the desire and/or courage to let go of an upset.*

Emotional Responsibility involves mastering both your thoughts and feelings, which is the express purpose of the 31 day programme in Section 2.

The computer
in your mind

Computer programmers use the expression "garbage in, garbage out" (or the acronym "GIGO") to refer to the fact that if you enter erroneous data into your computer, you will invariably obtain nonsensical output data.

The human mind operates in a similar manner. If your mind is programmed with negativity, scarcity and limiting beliefs, you will experience fear, difficulty and struggle in your life.

Of course, GIGO could also stand for "good in, good out"! If your mind is filled with thoughts of love, abundance and positivity, you will experience a happy, prosperous and joyful life.

The 31 day programme is like a software update, replacing negative, unresourceful beliefs with positive, resourceful ones. When you are feeling upset or stressed, you can use it to give yourself a fresh start!

POSITIVE
AFFIRMATIONS

> "
> *Since it will take time to absorb the affirmations in Section 2, we strongly recommend that you focus on only one per day.*
> "

What is an
affirmation?

An affirmation is a positive statement that you use to improve the quality of your life.

Most of the affirmations in this book have three important qualities:

① *They are worded in the first person singular.*

② *They are stated in the present tense.*

③ *They are positive statements, not double negatives.*

For example, in the affirmation "I am smart enough":

① *The word "I" is first person singular.*

② *The word "am" is present tense, as opposed to future tense, "will be".*

③ *The word "smart" is positive, as opposed to the double negative, "not stupid".*

Most affirmations possess these three qualities.

How to use
affirmations

Here are some suggestions on how to gain the maximum benefit from the affirmations in this book.

1 Like a carpenter learning to use a range of tools, you will learn a new affirmation every day for thirty-one days. Reflect upon each affirmation and explore its meaning. Since it will take time to absorb the affirmations, we strongly recommend that you work through them sequentially, focusing on only one per day.

2 You may repeat a day if you feel the affirmation is of particular value to you, but don't skip pages. Work your way through every affirmation, even if you think some of them are not relevant to you. You may be surprised how effective they are, because the affirmations are speaking to your unconscious mind.

3 The best time to use an affirmation is when you are feeling uncertain, anxious or upset. Keep using them for as long as it takes until the feeling subsides. Once you have read all thirty-one affirmations, you will have a repertoire from which to choose the one most relevant for you in a particular situation. For example, if you are running late for a meeting, you could say, "I always have enough time", or if you are feeling overwhelmed by the number of bills you are receiving, you could use the affirmation, "I always have enough money".

4 Some people try using affirmations, but give up after a short period of time because they think they're not working. The key is commitment and repetition. We recommend saying each affirmation at least seven times in succession. By saying them a number of times, you will eventually experience the benefit. Like rain falling onto dry ground, it takes a while for the information to soak into the deeper layers of your mind. Be persistent!

5 You may find that affirmations are best said aloud. Feel each word as you say it. Use the tone of voice that best embodies the meaning of the affirmation. For example, suppose you are saying the affirmation, "Because I am truly powerful, I always speak my truth." If this were true for you, what sort of person would you be? Surely you would be secure and self-assured. Your tone of voice would be confident, natural and matter-of-fact.

6 Play with the affirmations. Use different voices and act them out. You may enjoy reading them with a friend. Have fun! Millions of people have successfully used affirmations to improve their lives and so can you!

Fun Ways To Use Affirmations

Send yourself a text message with an affirmation.

Send yourself an email with an affirmation as the subject.

Make a computer desktop image with some affirmations.

Write an affirmation in lipstick on your bathroom mirror.

Leave an affirmation as a voice message on your phone.

Write affirmations on business cards and put them in your wallet.

Sing an affirmation in the shower.

Meditate on some affirmations.

Repeat your favourite affirmation as you are falling asleep.

Repeat affirmations mentally in time with the clickety-clack of train tracks.

Say an affirmations in time with your swimming strokes.

Say affirmations in time with your steps when walking.

Repeat an affirmation as a rap, while tapping the rhythm on a desk or your legs.

Whisper an affirmation.

Make the affirmations your computer screensaver.

When stuck in traffic, turn on the radio and sing affirmations to the melody of the songs.

Stare at an affirmation silently for sixty seconds.

Say some affirmations while looking at yourself in the bathroom mirror.

Write one affirmation for each day of your diary or electronic planner.

When you have finished reading this book, open the book at a random page. What relevance does that page have to your current life?

Shout an affirmation at the top of your voice.

Repeat an affirmation while waiting for a bus or appointment.

Close your eyes and visualise the words of an affirmation.

Write an affirmation ten times.

Record some affirmations and put them on your mp3 player.

Get a custom-made t-shirt with your favourite affirmation.

Write some affirmations on a poster and put it on a wall.

SECTION 2

THE 31 DAY
PROGRAMME

DAY 1

I am kind, gentle and patient with myself.

Many people think that they are not good enough or have, in some way, failed to fulfil their own expectations or those of their parents.

How can you rise above this type of thinking? First, you must understand that you are the innocent product of your life's circumstances, which include your genetics, ancestry, the economic and social circumstances of your childhood and the personalities of your parents.

Be kind, gentle and patient with yourself. Let go of any self-criticism, so you can make your life work and find the happiness you deserve.

DAY 2

I accept what's happening, no matter what I think and feel.

Your Personality has been formed by the interaction of forces and events you have experienced in your life. Many of these events are beyond your control and often outside of your awareness, but they are all operating within the laws of nature. Your life's circumstances are the feedback that you are receiving from the sum total of these forces.

Accepting your current situation does not necessarily mean that you want things to remain the same. Rather, acceptance removes your feeling of frustration and sense of injustice.

Trust that life works. Things are always as they should be and if something is out of balance, there is something for you to learn, without invalidating yourself, other people or the circumstances you are experiencing. This enables you to be open and to learn, grow and be happy.

DAY 3

I feel great!

When it's a cold, overcast day, do you find yourself thinking, "What a gloomy day" and feeling a bit down?

When you think you're running out of time to complete the tasks on your to-do list, do you feel overwhelmed?

Do you sometimes wake up feeling fat or tired? Do you ever feel that you're old or ugly?

When these thoughts enter your mind, it's easy to succumb to your feelings. However, these are clearly not helpful ways of thinking and feeling.

When you're feeling bad, stop whatever you're doing for a moment. Relax by closing your eyes, taking a deep breath and affirming, "I feel great!" at least ten times. If you repeat this affirmation enough times with conviction, it will quickly change the way you feel and turn your day around.

The quality of your life is not determined by what is actually happening around you, but how you choose to feel about what you are experiencing in the present moment.

DAY 4

I keep what I need and release what I don't.

Life is a balance between assimilation and elimination: physically, mentally and emotionally. Today's affirmation works on all three levels. It instructs your unconscious mind to keep what is useful for you and release what is no longer useful.

On a physical level, this affirmation is great for losing weight. By repeating it, you are instructing your body to only assimilate that part of your food intake that is appropriate for your well-being and to eliminate that which is not. Of course, it is still helpful to pay attention to your calorie intake and level of exercise, but your mental attitude and emotional state are significant factors in the amount of weight you carry.

Spring cleaning is a liberating experience. Clearing your clutter improves your physical environment and frees your mental space. If you haven't worn a piece of clothing for more than a year, why not donate it to charity?

On a mental level, this affirmation can relate to your belief system. While it's valuable to keep the beliefs that are working for you and creating happiness, it's equally important to release any beliefs that create unhappiness.

On an emotional level, this affirmation helps you to release old feelings of regret, resentment, jealousy and so on, while keeping your natural feelings of love, joy and peace with yourself and others.

DAY 5

I am smart enough.
I am attractive enough.
I am good enough.

Do you feel you are smart enough? Most traditional education systems use a "best" to "worst" ranking scale. The unfortunate consequence is that many people are conditioned into believing that they are not smart enough.

Everyone is talented, but traditional schooling systems only measure a limited range of academic parameters. They often don't recognise or measure a wide range of human talents such as creative and artistic abilities, lateral and intuitive thinking, people and leadership skills, emotional intelligence, common sense and business flair.

Do you feel you are attractive enough? The fashion industry and the media love to portray the "perfect" face and body and hold it up as the ideal. We are led to believe that if we don't measure up to that ideal, we are not attractive enough.

Everyone is attractive. When you are healthy and happy, your inner beauty shines through and others will be attracted to you.

Your self-worth is not dependent on external factors, such as your appearance or your material, social, professional or academic status. Furthermore, your self-worth is not dependent on other people's opinions or your ability to achieve.

You are already worthy, purely by virtue of your existence. You are good enough, right here and now. Your destiny is to claim your own authority over yourself.

DAY 6

I always have enough time.

One of the greatest causes of stress for many people is the self-limiting belief, "I do not have enough time". They project this belief into the future and unconsciously create and attract situations where they have too little time. Then they panic.

We all have 168 hours in each week. Nobody has any more or less time than you, so it's futile to complain about not having enough time. It's all about managing your time effectively.

The secret to managing your time is learning how to manage your anxiety relating to time. When you think that you don't have enough time, you have allowed yourself to be overwhelmed by your anxiety.

The next time you feel overwhelmed and think you have too much on your plate and not enough time to do it, take a deep breath and say several times to yourself, "I always have enough time". This will reduce your anxiety, which allows you to think more clearly and find ways of achieving your desired outcome in the available time.

DAY 7

I always have enough money.

Do you feel that life is a struggle because you never have enough money?

If you repeat today's affirmation every time you feel anxious about money until your anxiety subsides, you will eventually release all your anxiety about money.

Here are four keys to financial prosperity:

1 Always value your time, your contribution and yourself. You have a unique gift which you bring to this world.

2 Recognise that the world is abundant and that you can have what you want and need. You really can be wealthy, without depleting the world's natural resources or depriving others of their needs. Prosperity is a result of thinking holistically, whereas scarcity and struggle are the result of limited thinking and not recognising the consequences to yourself and others of your actions.

3 Understand that it is fair and ethical for you to be prosperous as your reward for your contribution to society. Have integrity, be honest and keep to your agreements. You deserve to have what you want. Ask for it!

4 Adopt an attitude of gratitude. For example, when paying bills, be grateful for the services and products you have purchased. When you view the glass as half full, it will fill!

DAY 8

I am unique, special and extraordinary.

You don't need to strive to be special and unique, because you already are! There is no one else like you. You have extraordinary qualities and talents that this world needs.

But it's a paradox. When you realise how unique, special and extraordinary you are, it's no big deal! The trick is to not let it go to your head and become conceited or arrogant.

Once you accept how special you are, you will understand that you are a part of something greater than yourself and you will experience a deep sense of gratitude and humility.

All so-called "ordinary people" are actually amazing, fabulous and extraordinary.

DAY 9

I accept myself just as I am.

We can often be harsh on ourselves. We can be tough taskmasters in what we expect of ourselves and often see ourselves as failing to fulfil our own expectations.

An important key to being happy is to accept yourself as you are, with all your perceived foibles and shortcomings. If a piece of software in your computer is faulty, you don't throw out your computer, you just fix the software.

In the same way, just because you want to improve your behaviour, you don't have to think of yourself as being bad or wrong. Thinking of yourself as bad or wrong only makes it harder to improve your behaviour.

Self-acceptance is one of life's greatest achievements and is far more valuable and significant than material success. Interestingly, self-acceptance is often a stepping-stone to greater material success.

DAY 10

I choose love and acceptance all day, today.

At any moment, you have two choices: you can either accept or reject your life's circumstances.

Rejection of your circumstances creates confusion and pain. If you think, "Damn, I don't need this in my life" or "Why me?", you are saying that those experiences should not be occurring and that something is wrong. This type of thinking creates unhappiness.

When you reject the feedback that life is offering you, you miss the opportunity to learn and grow. It's like ignoring the oil pressure warning light flashing on your car's dashboard - if you keep thinking like that, your engine will blow up!

Acceptance, on the other hand, creates ease and flow and also implies that your life is as it should be. However, in the short term, accepting certain situations may be uncomfortable, because you are changing old habits.

When you accept your life's circumstances, you begin to see how you created them, what you need to learn and how to improve your life. In the long term, acceptance makes your life operate easily and effortlessly.

DAY 11

I always accept other people just the way they are.

How do you feel when you believe that someone is being rude to you? How do you feel when someone appears to lack common sense? How do you feel when someone behaves in a strange and inexplicable way?

A common response is to think of that person as stupid or rude and be frustrated or annoyed. If you go down that road, you are not going to be happy and you are likely to become stupid and ignorant yourself!

So how can you still be happy when someone is behaving in an unacceptable manner? Well, you may not be able to change another person's behaviour, but you can change your attitude and feelings about that person. When you can be emotionally neutral while someone is being inconsiderate of your feelings, you liberate yourself from the effect of their behaviour.

As you affirm, "I always accept other people just the way they are", the cloud of your frustration diminishes and your tolerance and happiness flourish.

DAY 12

My upset is an opportunity to learn and grow.

Your ultimate goal is to be happy and at peace with yourself and your life, but along the way things will happen that may not be pleasant or comfortable. Do you ever feel angry, disappointed, sad, hurt, rejected, frustrated, confused, betrayed, afraid or resentful? When feeling these emotions, many people blame other people or external circumstances and fail to see their role in manifesting the drama.

In any drama, you can either adopt victim, aggressor or creator consciousness. Victims believe that they are suffering due to circumstances beyond their control. Aggressors believe they have to defend themselves against a dangerous world and thus believe that "offence is the best form of defence". Creators accept responsibility for the circumstances of their life and in turn create the life that they desire. Which role do you wish to play?

When operating from creator consciousness, you recognise that when you feel upset, your buttons are being pressed and you are simply receiving feedback from your unconscious mind.

The first step in releasing a victim/aggressor pattern is to be aware that it is your own mind that is creating your upset. You then have two ways to eliminate your upset. You could ask yourself why you feel upset, until you recognise that your upset is because you have a limiting belief about yourself and then choose to be kind and supportive to yourself. Alternatively, you could simply sit still in a quiet place with your eyes closed and focus on your breathing until your anxiety disappears.

DAY 13

I am surrounded by people who love and support me.

You already have a great deal of goodwill and support from your family, friends, colleagues and even strangers.

However, if the source of love and support is not obvious to you, then you must be blocking it consciously or unconsciously. This happens when, on some level, you feel unworthy or are being critical or defensive. Without knowing it, you may be pushing away the very love and support that you need.

Develop an attitude of gratitude towards others and it will create more opportunities and circumstances for you to be loved and supported.

When you choose to believe that you are surrounded by people who love and support you, you will attract more love and support into your life.

DAY 14

I live in the present moment and let my future take care of itself.

Do you ever worry about your future? Are you anxious about the state of the economy, your finances or job security? Do you worry about the future for members of your family?

There is a difference between planning for the future and worrying about the future. When planning for the future, you are deciding on your direction and even taking practical steps to make it happen.

However, when you worry, you are unconsciously choosing to be afraid of the future and believing that it will not be okay. If your aim is to be happy, why on earth would you choose to believe that?

Most of what people worry about never actually happens! When you learn to stop worrying, not only will your quality of life improve significantly, but you will also begin to create better outcomes in your life.

A key to being happy is to do your best in the present moment with the knowledge and resources available to you and let your future take care of itself.

The only reality that exists is the present moment! The future is just a projection from the present moment. The past is only a recollection in the present moment of an event that has occurred.

By focusing your attention in the present moment, you are in your most resourceful state.

DAY 15

I live a fabulous, fantastic and fortunate life.

When Anton arrived at a conference with his eight-year-old daughter Sophia, he was told that his presentation had been delayed an hour.

To pass the time, he took Sophia outside for a walk along a busy road. He was feeling hot and frustrated, which was exacerbated by the belching traffic fumes and noise.

Meanwhile, Sophia was picking daisies from the nature strip along the footpath. As Anton noticed her beautiful posy of flowers, she commented, "Daddy, look at the ant road" and pointed to a crack running along a brick wall, where a trail of ants was travelling. Suddenly all his frustration and negativity evaporated. He could see the magic that she was seeing.

Your perception of life is all in your mind. Every moment of every day brings new experiences and new opportunities. Life is magical. Look for the magic in your life, because it's all around you. What magic are you experiencing in this moment, right now?

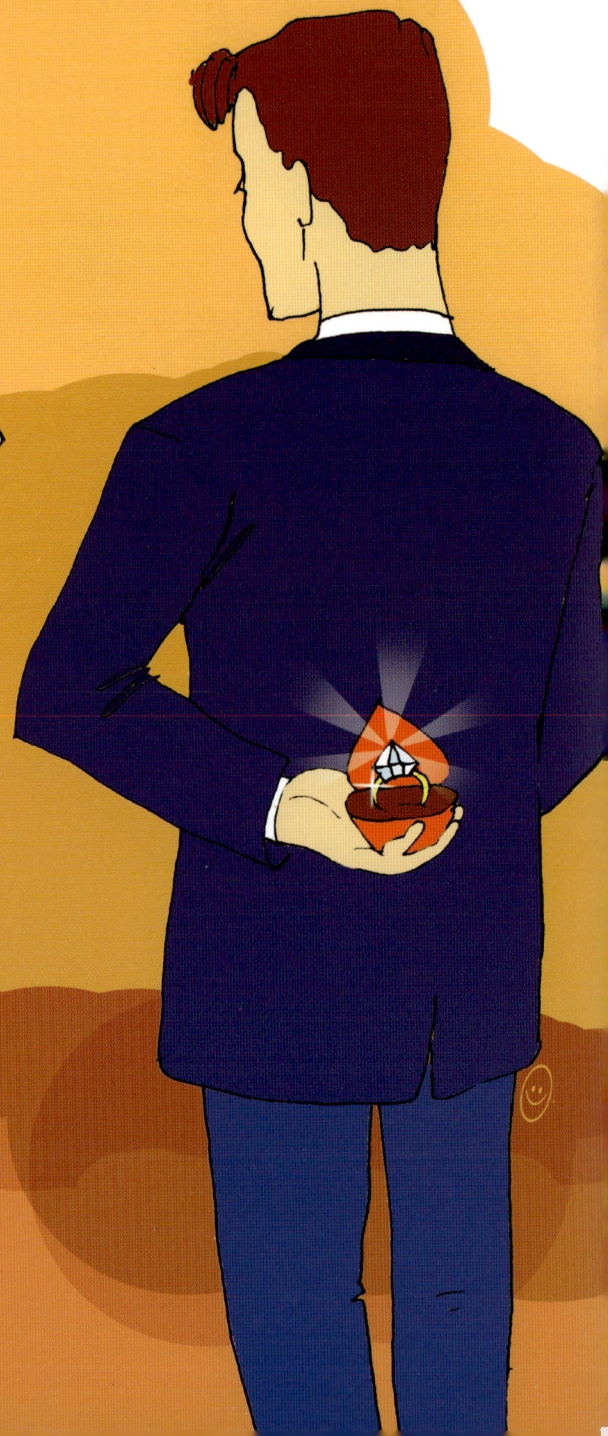

DAY 16

I know nothing.
I make no decisions.
I've forgotten the question!

This affirmation is a reminder that we must be careful not to jump to conclusions.

Michael has used this affirmation with great success many times when counselling clients who are feeling very distressed, and has found that it usually calms them down quickly. If you try to analyse it rationally, it may make no sense. However, the reason it is so effective is that it speaks directly to your unconscious mind.

In relaxed circumstances, if there is a problem, then thinking about it and working out a solution is a rational, effective strategy. But when you are overly anxious, you are not in the frame of mind to find a solution.

Unconsciously, you could be anxious because you are afraid of failure. For example, you may be afraid of not being accepted for the job you really want. Alternatively, you could be afraid of the outcome of a decision, such as leaving a long-term relationship.

This is when thinking about a situation is not the best way to move forward, because it is the act of thinking that is contributing to your anxiety and you are suffering from analysis paralysis. Your first priority is to change how you are feeling. Calm down and chill out, before you start to think about your situation.

Practise switching off your mind. An easy way to do this is to focus on deep breathing, as you inhale and exhale through your nose.

Today's affirmation has been adapted from the book "A Course In Miracles" and is best used when you are feeling distressed.

DAY 17

I'm okay even if I don't feel okay.

Sometimes life may seem dark, gloomy and even scary.

At times like these, you may feel upset and over-whelmed by your emotions. However, it's important to remember that a feeling is just a chemical reaction taking place in your body.

When you are feeling upset, you have two choices. You can choose to believe that what you are feeling is justified and continue to feel upset. Alternatively, you can choose to not give your power away to your feelings, by making a decision to feel okay, which will trigger endorphins to be released into your body and soon you will feel okay.

A great way to deal with anxiety is to sit or lie down for five to ten minutes, close your eyes, focus on your breathing and remain still. Your muscles will relax, your blood pressure and adrenal glands will normalise and the cloud of uncertainty will evaporate.

DAY 18

I love them and they love me.

When Terry was sharing an apartment with his friend Julie, they would go for early morning power walks around their local bay. The first time he walked with her, he noticed that she said, "Good morning" to everyone they passed. They passed more than fifty people and at least twenty ignored her.

Terry asked, "Why are you doing this, when so many people are ignoring you?" to which Julie replied, "I feel safer when I know the people in my neighbourhood and they know me" and kept on greeting everyone she met. By the end of the week, everyone was responding enthusiastically to her greeting and treating her as a friend.

Our greatest need as human beings is for connection. Love really does make the world go round.

The next time you feel disconnected from someone, try thinking, "I love them and they love me" a few times and believe it. Then watch the magic that happens.

DAY 19

*I don't have to believe every thought I think.
I choose to believe the thoughts that empower
me and others.*

Do you believe any of the following?

"There are no good men (or women) out there."

"Women (or men) are always trying to take advantage of you."

"You have to be careful, because people are trying to rip you off."

"It's hard to make a lot of money honestly."

"It's a dangerous world out there."

"I can't depend on anyone except myself."

"Exams are stressful."

For many people these beliefs seem so real that they appear to be how the world really is. But are these perspectives useful? Are there better ways to view the world?

Most thinking is habitual and often limiting. The problem is that self-limiting beliefs ultimately create right and wrong, good and bad, winners and losers, and thus lead to unhappiness.

To be happy, you must first recognise your limiting beliefs and opt out of them. Decide which beliefs you choose to have and which ones to reject.

DAY 20

I accept myself in the presence of others.

Many people tremble at the very thought of speaking to an audience. In fact, numerous surveys have shown that for most people, their fear of public speaking is even greater than their fear of death.

Why are people so afraid of public speaking? Quite simply, it is their fear of being judged by others. Ironically, they are only afraid of being judged by others because they have already judged themselves as being somehow inadequate!

Most of the time, other people are too busy thinking about themselves to be thinking about you. Relax and affirm, "I accept myself in the presence of others."

When you accept yourself, others will accept you.

DAY 21

I choose harmony.

When two people have a difference of opinion, an argument often develops. This is because we have been conditioned by society to believe that things are either right or wrong. As a consequence, each person feels that they must defend their position. Otherwise they think that they will be perceived to be "wrong", "lose face" and suffer defeat.

Unfortunately, with this way of thinking, you may win the argument but still not be happy! When you are arguing with someone, there is a subtext - you are usually seeking respect and/or recognition.

There is a much better way to feel happy and validated. Rather than needing to prove yourself, recognise that you actually have nothing to prove, as you already are special and unique. Not only that, the person you are conversing with is also special and unique. Neither of you has anything to prove.

What you are both experiencing is just a difference of opinion – and differences of opinion are valuable, because they offer an alternative perspective and the opportunity to develop tolerance, humility and compassion. You can choose to be happy and create harmony, then figure out whether your perspective is helpful or not.

DAY 22

The more powerful I become, the more gently I behave.

Truly powerful people are not struggling or forcing. They are in harmony with the people and circumstances around them.

The three positions of personal power are victim, aggressor and creator.

1 The victim is at the mercy of circumstances and feels powerless to change their environment.

2 The aggressor is dominating and forceful, which is the position many people perceive as being powerful.

3 The creator is a person who is truly powerful, as they have their life's circumstances the way they wish them to be, without struggle or force.

Let's look at how these three positions might apply in the workplace:

The victim is afraid of losing her job, but doesn't enjoy it and complains about the work and people. Although she has financial security, her fundamental needs are not being met. She feels taken advantage of and is not happy.

The aggressor is a bully. She is competitive, domineering, impatient and sees her colleagues as incompetent and inefficient. She is meeting her need to feel superior but is fighting, struggling and still unhappy.

The creator loves her job and feels empowered, fulfilled and valued. She is sensitive to the needs of her colleagues and clients, while remaining clear about what she wants and how to go about getting it. She is happy, fulfilled and empowered. This is a win-win position.

True power comes from understanding the ethical and practical principles of life and acting on that knowledge. Clarity leads to power, not force or wilfulness. When you are clear, you act at the right time, with the least effort, to the greatest effect. The more powerful you become, the more gently you will behave.

DAY 23

Because I am truly powerful, I always speak my truth.

Truly powerful people do not pretend, tell lies or use emotional blackmail. They are authentic, honest and real to themselves and others. They are willing to take a risk, stand by their convictions and be emotionally vulnerable. For example, they are prepared to admit that they are wrong or have made a mistake.

Being emotionally vulnerable includes being prepared to reveal your fears and doubts. Many people believe that protecting themselves is a good strategy for staying safe. If we are talking about protecting yourself from physical harm, that may be true, but when it comes to emotional danger, protecting yourself often creates the opposite effect.

Are you afraid of confrontation, because you think it may create argument, misunderstanding or rejection? By avoiding confrontation, the underlying issue may not be addressed and you may create other issues that in time grow out of hand.

The good intention in avoiding confrontation is to create harmony, but if it is purely based on a fear of conflict, it may ultimately create disharmony.

Truly powerful people are open, honest and transparent. They are also prepared to feel fear, take emotional risks, while still being considerate towards others.

Facing and moving through your fears creates confidence and ultimately leads to happiness.

DAY 24

I am open-hearted, even around closed-hearted people.

Debbie was renovating her kitchen. She purchased some prefabricated cabinets but, when they were delivered, discovered that some of the parts were missing. Feeling frustrated, she went back to the store and accused them of ripping her off. An argument erupted, with each party accusing the other of wrongdoing. Only after a long struggle did the store finally agree to provide the missing parts.

Roger had also been renovating his kitchen and a similar mistake had occurred with the delivery from his supplier. At first, the company was reluctant to admit they had made a mistake, but Roger remained calm, sympathetic and open-hearted. He recognised the time pressure the staff were operating under and expressed his gratitude for all they had done to date. They apologised for their mistake and said the missing parts would be delivered to Roger the next day, at their cost.

Protecting yourself by behaving defensively will often be misinterpreted by other people as being rude, uncaring, aggressive or a covert attack. You can significantly lessen misunderstanding and improve your chances of achieving your desired outcome by staying open-hearted around closed-hearted people.

DAY 25

I always have the right people to support me.

Do you ever feel that you are surrounded by incompetent people? Do you find it difficult to communicate with certain people? Do you ever think that people are fundamentally selfish?

While it's true that there are some people who are incompetent and hard to communicate with, a more useful question to ask yourself is, "Why am I experiencing this kind of treatment from these people?".

The behaviour of these people may be a result of your tendency to judge others. When you let go of your judgment, you may be pleasantly surprised by the positive change in their behaviour. You see, people are mirrors of your inner nature. They reflect back to you both the good and bad aspects of yourself.

By seeing the good in others, they will see the good in you. As you repeat the affirmation, "I always have the right people to support me", you will attract into your life new people who respect and support you. Furthermore, the people already around you will treat you with more respect and support.

DAY 26

I trust life and the processes of life.

Valerie was expecting her first child. Because it was two weeks overdue, she was worried that if the baby were not born within the next few days, it would have to be induced or delivered by Caesarean section and she feared the worst.

She booked a session with her counsellor to see if her anxiety was delaying the birth of her baby. By working through issues from her early childhood, it was revealed that Valerie had been a fearful child and had taken on her mother's belief that the world is a dangerous place.

The counsellor helped Valerie to release her fear and adopt an attitude of acceptance, knowing that whatever happened, she would be okay and able to cope with it. He helped her learn to trust life and the processes of life.

The next day, Valerie experienced a long and difficult labour. Although her worst fears were realised when she did need a Caesarean, she remained calm, positive and trusting throughout the ordeal. Valerie allowed life to flow through her and, because she believed her child was safe, her baby was born healthy and relaxed.

We can either see the world as a chaotic, dangerous place with no justice or purpose, or we can see it as a magical, intelligent, benevolent place.

Both realities exist. Which do you choose?

DAY 27

I live in a safe, loving and abundant world.

The visionary American philosopher and engineer Buckminster Fuller stated in his ground-breaking book "Critical Path" that, from his research, there are enough resources on Earth for every human being to live to the standard of a billionaire, without depleting the Earth's natural resources.

So why is there is such a wide spectrum of social and material realities on our planet, from suffering and great poverty, to total love and abundance?

The level of love and abundance that you experience in your life is mostly related to the set of beliefs you have inherited. When you accept responsibility for your life's circumstances, without blaming yourself or others, you can focus on transforming your unresourceful beliefs to more resourceful ones.

The easiest way to improve your level of prosperity is to focus on the abundance and love that already exists in your life.

By repeating today's affirmation faithfully, you will experience a greater feeling of security in your life and you will ultimately prosper!

DAY 28

I am whole and connected to myself, others and the world around me.

There have been a number of musicians and celebrities who have achieved enormous success, fame and wealth, yet have still felt lost and alone. In an attempt to ease their pain, they have turned to sex, alcohol and drugs, which ultimately killed them.

For people who seemingly had more than most people can only dream of, why were they so unhappy? How much does one really need to achieve or acquire to be truly happy? What is the essence of true happiness?

Addictive behaviour is an attempt to alleviate the feeling of loneliness. This includes both substance addiction (such as the need for alcohol, nicotine, caffeine, prescription or illegal drugs and over-eating) and process addiction (such as being a workaholic, gym junkie, sex addict, computer games fanatic, television addict or anything that involves compulsive behaviour).

But not everyone who enjoys a glass of wine or a cup of coffee is an addict. It's when you have a craving for it and feel you can't do without it, that it is useful to examine your need for it.

The antidote for loneliness is connectedness. To feel connected is as simple as making the decision to be connected to oneself and others. Everywhere we turn, there are people who will love and support us, if we just open our hearts to feel it.

Your happiness does not depend on what you own or what you do. Your happiness is an intrinsic quality of your existence. It comes from feeling whole and connected to yourself, others and the world around you.

DAY 29

I let go of my past and live in the present moment.

Do you have regrets or feel guilty about things you said or did in your past? Do you wish you could change aspects of your past? Do you believe that what happened to you in the past may happen again in the future?

Many people have fears and limitations because of their past, but what exactly is "your past"? Your past is simply your present-time interpretation of events that have taken place in your life.

You can't change what has already happened, but you can change how you think and feel about those events. It is your choice whether you continue to

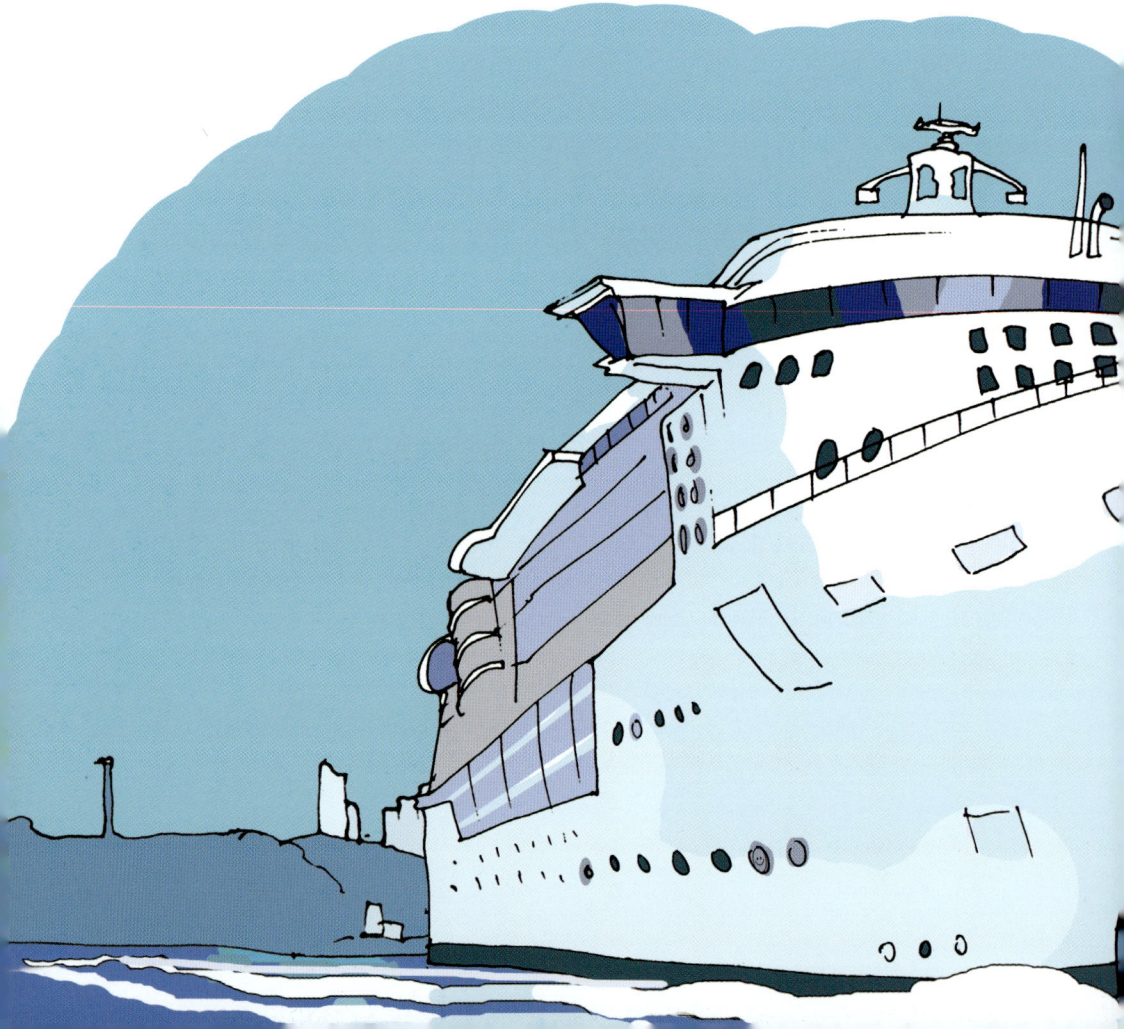

interpret those events in a positive or negative way. As William Shakespeare wisely wrote, "there is nothing either good or bad, but thinking makes it so".

Did people say or do things in your past that were hurtful to you? Are you willing to forgive them? Have you ever said or done things that were hurtful to others? Are you willing to forgive yourself?

By forgiving yourself and others, you liberate yourself and live in the present moment. When you choose to live in the present moment, then, in this moment, there are no past fears and limitations.

DAY 30

I always have enough love.

When I look with eyes of love, love finds me.
Love touches and embraces me.
Love lifts me and kisses me.
Love sometimes challenges me and frightens me,
But love always excites me.

Love is my beginning, middle and end.
Love is the reason I am here.
Love is beyond the mind.

I forgive myself for not trusting love.
I surrender to love with all of my being.

Love is all-encompassing and all-fulfilling.
Love is whole and complete.
There is only love.
I am love.

DAY 31

I am always safe, connected and accepted.

This is an all-inclusive affirmation that addresses the three primal self-limiting beliefs of Adamedes' Triad, which are revealed in Section 3.

It is your birthright to lead a secure, prosperous life, filled with love and joy, every moment of every day.

Congratulations for working through the thirty-one affirmations!

Which days would you like to revisit, to reinforce your new, more enlightened outlook on life?

SECTION 3

ADAMEDES'
TRIAD OF PRIMAL
SELF-LIMITING
BELIEFS

DISCOVERY
OF ADAMEDES'
TRIAD

> 66 *By 2004, Michael concluded that all self-limiting beliefs can be grouped into one or more of three categories.* 99

Since the early twentieth century, psychologists have been studying human beings' self-limiting beliefs, in an attempt to free their clients from limiting thoughts and behaviours.

Michael Adamedes began his counselling practice in 1982. Inspired by the work of many influential thinkers, in particular the American psychiatrist and author David Hawkins, Michael sought to simplify the understanding of his clients' issues and then broaden his discoveries to encompass all of humanity's self-limiting thinking.

In line with the principle of Occam's Razor, which advocates choosing the simplest explanation for a phenomenon, Michael claims, "The truth is simple".

He believes that by reducing a process to its essential elements, we have more understanding and power over it.

By 2004, after counselling thousands of clients, Michael concluded that all self-limiting beliefs can be grouped into one or more of the following three categories of primal self-limiting beliefs:

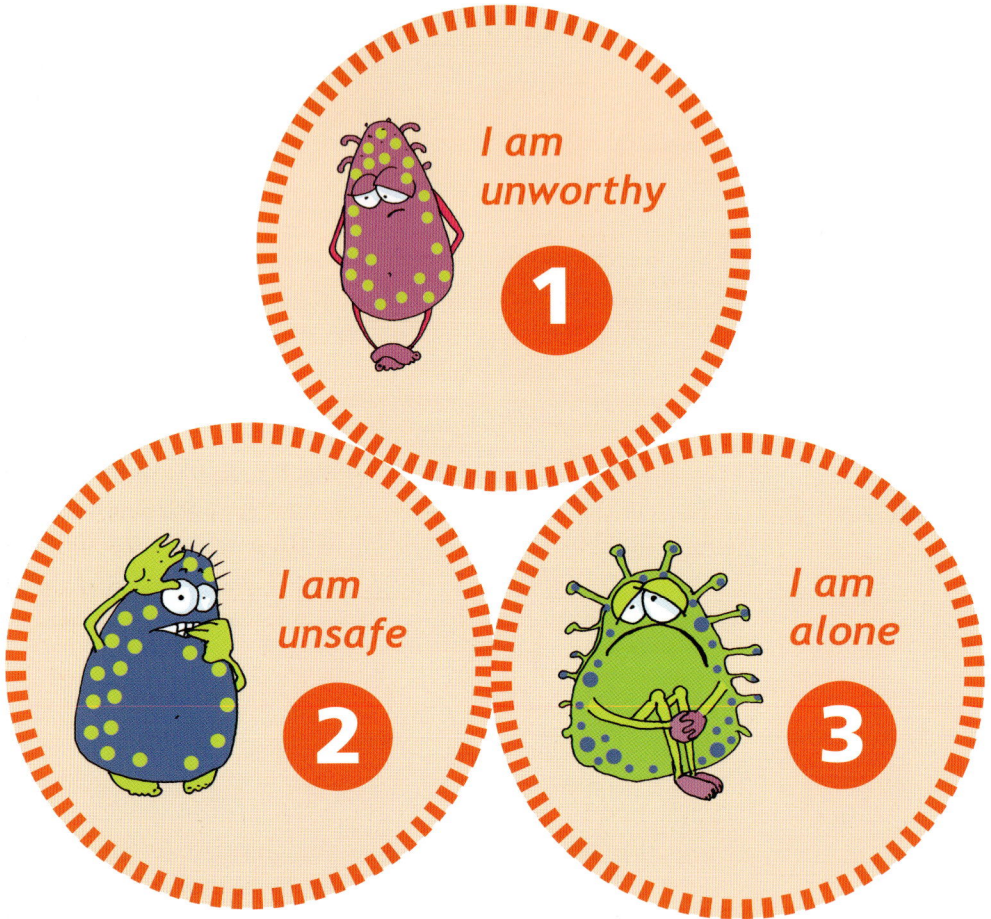

All emotional pain is created by subscribing to one or more of these beliefs.

Your self-limiting beliefs can be thought of as bacteria that have invaded your mind. Just as bacteria can be treated with antibiotics, self-limiting beliefs can be eliminated by using positive affirmations.

When experiencing a feeling of being unworthy, unsafe or alone, most people act out a compensatory behaviour. Compensatory behaviours can be passive or active. The following pages outline the most common compensatory behaviour for each category and the relevant remedial affirmations.

PRIMAL SELF-LIMITING BELIEF 1:
"I AM UNWORTHY"

"I am unworthy" is the first of the three primal self-limiting beliefs.

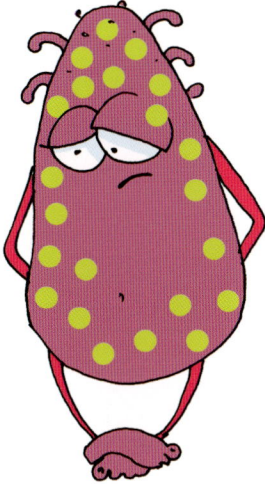

Many of us have grown up to believe that we are not good enough, undeserving of love or that there is something wrong with us. We may feel that we are inferior to other people or don't come from the right social or financial background. Perhaps we feel that we lack the intelligence, skills or abilities that are needed to succeed.

Do you sometimes feel that you are too fat, too short or not attractive enough? Are you embarrassed about your sexual orientation, or do you feel that you are from the wrong racial group? Are you ashamed about not having enough education or being too poor? All of these issues arise from the belief that you are unworthy.

"I am unworthy":
Passive compensatory behaviour

The passive compensatory behaviour that people often display when they believe that they are unworthy is to withdraw from a situation.

For example, Annalise is a student who refrains from asking questions in class, because she is afraid of the teacher and other students laughing at her and thinking that she is dumb. So, in effect, she rejects herself before they have the opportunity to reject her. Unfortunately, by not asking questions, she sabotages her learning.

Jerome works in the Information Technology industry. He has not had a pay rise for two years, but is afraid to ask his boss for one, because he can't stand the thought of being refused and feeling rejected, which he believes would prove that he is not good enough.

Kevin is jealous because his girlfriend Carol has received a birthday gift from her ex-boyfriend, Gavin. Kevin suspects that Carol still cares for Gavin and he believes that Gavin must be better than him. Kevin's way of dealing with this is to sulk and not want to go out. Carol simply thinks that it was kind of Gavin to give her a gift and is happy to be with Kevin.

"I am unworthy":
Active compensatory behaviour

The active compensatory behaviour that people often display when they believe that they are unworthy is trying to be "perfect" - that is, always trying to do it right and worrying that they may get it wrong. These people often need validation from others.

For example, Emma is preparing to go out on a date and spends two hours getting ready. She washes and styles her hair, does her fingernails and plucks her eyebrows. She tries on three different tops, four skirts, five pairs of shoes and six accessories! All because she doubts herself and wants to be "perfect" so that her date will accept her.

Because Mrs Arnold felt that she never succeeded in life and felt unworthy, she wanted her son Jason to become a doctor and make her proud. So she constantly nagged him to study hard and make a success of his life. Now that Jason is a leading medical specialist, his mother boasts to her friends about how brilliant and successful her son is. Unfortunately, Jason is going through a mid-life crisis, as he had always aspired to be a movie director. He gave up his true aspirations in order to gain his mother's approval. Mrs Arnold feels successful but Jason feels unfulfilled and distant from his mother.

Harry, Tommy and Nigel are elated when their country's team wins a football match, as it validates their shared belief that they are superior. However, when their team loses, they go on a drunken rampage of destruction, as their unconscious belief that they are unworthy has been exposed.

Olga is gossiping with her workmates about their manager Roger and complains that he is weak and can't make effective decisions. Although it is true that Roger is non-assertive and an ineffective manager, Olga also lacks confidence in herself and is afraid to address these issues with him. Because Olga has the unconscious belief that she is unworthy, she chooses to be critical of her manager behind his back and is thus as ineffective as Roger.

Affirmations to dispel
the belief that you are unworthy

DAY	AFFIRMATION
1	I am kind, gentle and patient with myself.
5	I am smart enough. I am attractive enough. I am good enough.
8	I am unique, special and extraordinary.
9	I accept myself just as I am.
11	I always accept other people just the way they are.
15	I live a fabulous, fantastic and fortunate life.
19	I don't have to believe every thought I think. I choose to believe the thoughts that empower me and others.
20	I accept myself in the presence of others.
31	I am always safe, connected and accepted.

PRIMAL SELF-LIMITING BELIEF 2:
"I AM UNSAFE"

"I am unsafe" is the second of the three primal self-limiting beliefs.

Do you believe that the world is a dangerous place? Do you feel that people are trying to take advantage of you, or that anyone can be mugged and we need more police? Do you believe that you are at constant risk of being infected by germs and it's easy to catch a cold? Do you feel you can't trust anyone and that people are often trying to take advantage of you?

If you can relate to any of these, then you believe that you are unsafe in the world. These are the beliefs of someone who has victim consciousness and is afraid of becoming a "loser" in a win-lose game of life.

Do you believe there's a sucker born every minute? Do you believe that the best form of defence is offence? Do you always have to be the driver when you're in the car with your partner? Do you believe in "an eye for an eye and a tooth for a tooth"? Do you believe there's no justice in the world, so you need to take the law into your own hands? Do you feel the need to prove your point in an argument and always have the last say?

These are some of the beliefs and behaviours of people who have aggressor consciousness, in which they see themselves as needing to fight, to be a "winner" in a win-lose game.

It is common to alternate between victim and aggressor consciousness: sometimes being withdrawn and passive and at other times hostile and aggressive. By learning valuable lessons from both perspectives, it is possible to find an assertive yet still harmonious middle ground. This is similar to a pendulum that swings from side to side until it eventually comes to rest at its equilibrium position. We call the equilibrium position "creator consciousness", where you achieve your desired outcomes and see yourself and others as "winners" in a win-win game!

"I am unsafe":
Passive compensatory behaviour

The passive compensatory behaviour that people often display when they believe that they are unsafe is to not engage in situations that they perceive to be potentially threatening.

Shirley has a secure senior position as a secretary in a government department. After eight years, she has become jaded and unhappy with the office politics and policy changes and now finds her job demeaning and meaningless. She knows she is highly competent but is afraid to leave her job, because she believes that suitable positions are scarce. She feels stuck and her health is now suffering.

Samuel and his sister Lilith planned to travel on a group sightseeing tour around England for Christmas. After Samuel heard about the attempted aircraft hijacking in London, he cancelled his trip, because he felt unsafe about travelling to England. Lilith believed that it was safe to fly to England, so she proceeded with her plans and had a wonderful time.

Graeme has received his monthly credit card statement and is dismayed to discover that he is over his limit. He has seven days to pay, but puts the statement in his desk drawer and tries to forget about it. As a result, he fails to pay on time and is charged additional interest on his account.

Margaret lives on her own in a magnificent five-bedroom house. Her children have moved out and her husband died several years ago. She finds it hard to maintain such a large house and her children are encouraging her to downsize to a luxurious new apartment and inject much-needed funds into her bank account. But she is afraid to sell her house, because she doesn't like having to change her routine, even though she is often exhausted from cleaning the house and is struggling financially. This is all because she feels unsafe and doesn't want to engage in new and unfamiliar situations.

Not stepping out of one's comfort zone to participate in a new activity is usually a result of feeling unsafe. Many people avoid joining a gym, learning to dance or sing, or pursuing their dreams, simply because they feel unsafe.

"I am unsafe":
Active compensatory behaviour

The active compensatory behaviour that people often display when they believe that they are unsafe is attempting to be in control. This may involve over-planning, the inability to delegate, needing to always be in charge, telling lies, withholding information, manipulating people or stealing. People who exhibit this type of behaviour believe that they can't trust other people or life itself.

Brent is upset because his wife Cheryl has overspent on their weekly housekeeping budget. As primary income earner, he is worried about the constant pressure of paying the family bills and believes that Cheryl is irresponsible with money. Brent is so stressed that he is constantly short-tempered with Cheryl and his two children.

Lizzy needs to plan her life as much as possible, to know in advance where she is going, who she is going to meet and what is going to happen. Before going on a week's vacation, she plans her itinerary for each day and becomes anxious and frustrated if there are any disruptions to her plans. When her partner Johnny suggests some last-minute changes, she becomes irate and bossy towards him.

Edgar has a printing business in which he works twelve hours a day, six days a week. He has an apprentice, Peter, whom he constantly criticizes for being inept. Because of this, Peter doesn't get the opportunity to try different tasks or expand his skills, which would reduce Edgar's workload. By being a bully and attempting to be in control, Edgar finds himself overworked and stressed - and his life is out of control.

Terence is a real estate agent who attempts to manipulate a newly-married couple, Wendy and William. He plays on their fears of scarcity by telling them that his property is the only one available that matches their wish list. He also lies to them, telling them that another interested party has made an offer, so they need to make a counter-offer now to secure the property. Terence is a wheeler-dealer who is prepared to use any trick to make a quick buck. Even though he may secure the sale, his deceptive nature and need to be in control is creating a serious rift in his relationship with his wife and children and he has no real friends. People who know his true nature can't trust him.

Because these people perceive life as unsafe, they continue to gather evidence and unconsciously attract and create situations to prove to themselves that this is the nature of life. Once they choose to adopt the belief that the world is a safe and abundant place, they, like millions of other people, can live a safer, happier and easier life.

Affirmations to dispel
the belief that you are unsafe

DAY	AFFIRMATION
2	I accept what's happening, no matter what I think and feel.
6	I always have enough time.
7	I always have enough money.
12	My upset is an opportunity to learn and grow.
14	I live in the present moment and let my future take care of itself.
15	I live a fabulous, fantastic and fortunate life.
17	I'm okay even if I don't feel okay.
19	I don't have to believe every thought I think. I choose to believe the thoughts that empower me and others.
23	Because I am truly powerful, I always speak my truth.
26	I trust life and the processes of life.
27	I live in a safe, loving and abundant world.
29	I let go of my past and live in the present moment.
31	I am always safe, connected and accepted.

PRIMAL SELF-LIMITING BELIEF 3:
"I AM ALONE"

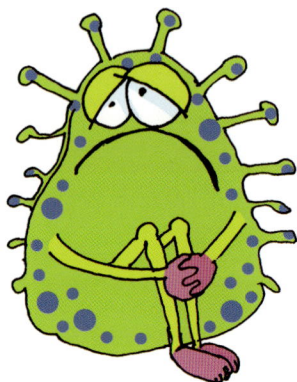

"I am alone" is the third and final primal self-limiting belief.

Do you find it difficult to be at home by yourself? Do you find it hard to sit still and do nothing? Do you find it hard to say goodbye to someone you love? Do you sometimes feel that you are all alone in this world and that there is no one you can depend on? Do you believe that in fact we are all alone?

All of these thoughts and feelings stem from the belief that you are alone. As explained earlier, the Personality is a self-induced hypnotic trance, one that is so convincing that many people never stop to think more deeply about why they experience certain emotions and situations or how to change them. By adopting more useful beliefs, you don't ever have to feel alone!

This deep-seated feeling of being alone is often caused by a lack of bonding with the mother. In the first year of your life, your mother represents the foundation of your existence. If you fail to bond with your mother, significant psychological and emotional imprints fail to occur in your mind and body, and you are left with a feeling of emptiness. As a child, this can result in a fear of being left alone, fear of the dark and fears of abandonment or of being lost. In adults, it can often lead to depression, compulsive behaviours, addictions and the breakdown of relationships.

Rather than being judgemental, it's important to understand why your mother may not have been able to be there for you. Maybe she wanted the connection with you but was overwhelmed by circumstances. She may not have been ready to have a baby at the time she fell pregnant with you, or perhaps she was ill during the pregnancy. There may have been some intervention during the birth process, where you and your mother were separated from each other for many hours after birth. Your mother may have been ill for a long time after your birth, or she may not have bonded with her own mother, in which case she may not have been able to fully bond with you.

Alternatively, your mother may have been emotionally and/or physically exhausted after having had too many children. If you were adopted or your mother died, you may have lost the opportunity to bond with your birth mother or a mother figure.

While other parental figures such as your father, grandparents, aunts, uncles, step-parents, a nanny or an adoptive parent can compensate for missed mothering, you don't actually need a parental substitute to overcome the lack of bonding with your mother. When you become aware of your issues, you can resolve them within yourself, such as through counselling, contemplation, journalling or the use of appropriate affirmations.

"I am alone":
Passive compensatory behaviour

The most common passive compensatory behaviour that people display when they believe that they are alone is to be withdrawn, isolated, easily bored and/or shut down, often resulting in depression.

Sixteen year-old Cameron finds it hard to make friends and spends most of his time watching television, listening to music and playing computer games. Because of his lack of social skills, he becomes increasingly more isolated and moody, rejecting his mother's attempts to introduce him to new friends. He is lonely, detached from his family and peers, deeply unhappy and depressed.

Joan refrains from going out and meeting new people because she feels alone and thinks no one can replace her deceased husband. She is afraid to fall in love again, fearing that a new partner would leave her and exacerbate her feelings of loneliness.

"I am alone":
Active compensatory behaviour

Some typical active compensatory behaviours that people display when they believe that they are alone are workaholism, the inability to sit still or be silent (and hence having the need for constant stimulation) and addiction to alcohol, drugs, sex or gambling.

Diana, who is seventeen, feels isolated and has become a rebel. She feels disconnected from her father, can't relate to her school teachers and is skipping classes. On weekends, she is a binge drinker, parties hard and is promiscuous. Karen is unhappy in her marriage and feels estranged from the man she once adored. To compensate for her feelings of deep loneliness and anxiety and to make herself feel better, she becomes a gym junkie. In an attempt to further escape from her loneliness, she becomes competitive at work and spends long hours at the office, but she still feels lonely.

In extreme situations, feelings of being alone can lead to depression and even thoughts of suicide.

Affirmations to dispel
the belief that you are alone

DAY	AFFIRMATION
10	I choose love and acceptance all day, today.
11	I always accept other people just the way they are.
13	I am surrounded by people who love and support me.
14	I live in the present moment and let my future take care of itself.
15	I live a fabulous, fantastic and fortunate life.

DAY	AFFIRMATION
18	I love them and they love me.
19	I don't have to believe every thought I think. I choose to believe the thoughts that empower me and others.
24	I am open-hearted, even around closed-hearted people.
25	I always have the right people to support me.
27	I live in a safe, loving and abundant world.
28	I am whole and connected to myself, others and the world around me.
29	I let go of my past and live in the present moment.
30	I always have enough love.
31	I am always safe, connected and accepted.

COMBINATION OF PRIMAL
SELF-LIMITING BELIEFS

You may have more than one self-limiting belief activated at the same time.

Here are all the possible combinations of primal self-limiting beliefs, along with a scenario in which each could occur and three ways of responding.

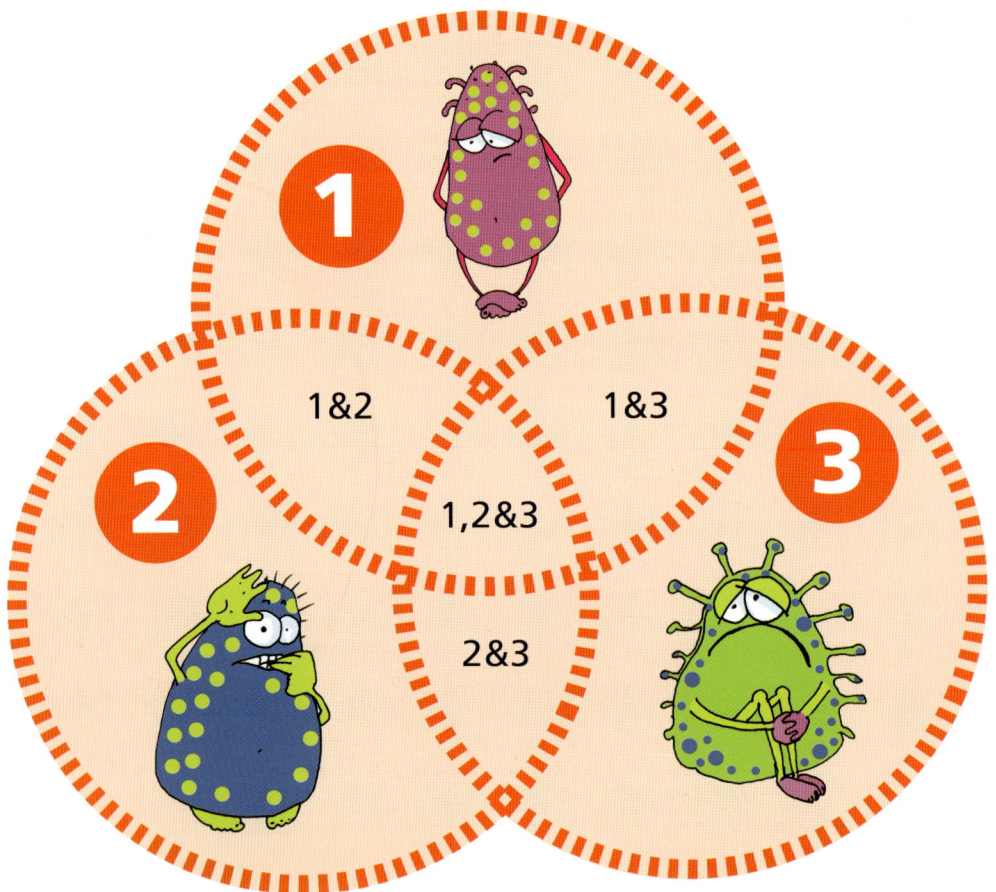

1

2

3

1&2

1&3

1,2&3

2&3

Primal Self-Limiting Beliefs 1 & 2:
"I am unworthy and unsafe"

Frida has been unemployed for some time and feels unworthy because she thinks she is a failure, and unsafe because she doesn't know how she is going to pay her bills.

Passive compensatory behaviour
She feels hopeless, becomes depressed and gives up looking for a job.

Active compensatory behaviour
She is angry, feels resentful and becomes obsessed with looking for a job.

Enlightened perspective
Frida recognises that the right job has not yet materialised and knows that it is only a matter of time before she finds it. In the meantime, she manages her anxiety about finding a job and paying her bills by using affirmations such as "I am unique, special and extraordinary" and "I always have enough money", while continuing to search for the right job.

Primal Self-Limiting Beliefs 1 & 3:
"I am unworthy and alone"

Five years ago, Lionel separated from his long-term girlfriend and he still hasn't found a new partner. He feels lonely and not deserving of being loved.

Passive compensatory behaviour
He loses hope, believes that there are no good women available and gives up trying to find a new girlfriend.

Active compensatory behaviour
He doesn't believe that any woman will ever truly love him and, although he has many one-night stands, he still feels lonely and unworthy.

Enlightened perspective
Lionel knows that he is a worthy, loving person and deserves a great relationship. He is open to finding the right person and focuses on becoming more considerate

towards others. To help himself through this period, he uses affirmations such as "I accept myself just as I am" and "I always have enough love".

Primal Self-Limiting Beliefs 2 & 3:
"I am unsafe and alone"

Gloria's husband has gone on an extended overseas business trip and she feels lonely and afraid of being alone in the house.

Passive compensatory behaviour
She feels sad, eats lots of chocolate, mindlessly watches television until late at night and double checks all the door and window locks before going to bed. These are passive behaviours, as she has isolated herself from the outside world and her feelings.

Active compensatory behaviour
She constantly goes out with her friends and is never at home on her own. However, she still feels unsafe and lonely.

Enlightened perspective
Gloria uses affirmations such as "I live in a safe, loving and abundant world" and "I am surrounded by people who love and support me". As a result, she has an extensive network of friends and enjoys their company, but is equally happy to stay home at night on her own, and renews her interest in playing the piano.

Primal Self-Limiting Beliefs 1, 2 & 3:
"I am unworthy, unsafe and alone"

Albert's wife has left him for another man and he now feels unloved, lonely and financially insecure because they have to sell their family home.

Passive compensatory behaviour
He becomes depressed and drinks alcohol to excess in an attempt to escape from his feelings.

Active compensatory behaviour

He is angry, feels betrayed and blames his wife for leaving him. He works out excessively at the gym and is now dating a woman twenty years younger than himself, to prove that he is strong and desirable, but still feels anxious about life.

Enlightened perspective

Albert realises that he was in a loveless relationship for many years and that he was too afraid to do anything about it. Even though he sometimes feels overwhelmed with fear, he knows that he now has a chance to overcome his fear and find a truly loving partner. He affirms, "I let go of my past and live in the present moment" and "I live in a safe, loving and abundant world". To reduce his anxiety, he affirms "I know nothing. I make no decisions. I have forgotten the question!".

SUMMARY OF COMMON
COMPENSATORY BEHAVIOURS

The table below shows some common behaviours that people act out in an attempt to compensate for each of the three primal self-limiting beliefs.

This table is not definitive, as there may be more than one possible self-limiting belief that underlies a particular behaviour.

By becoming aware of these self-sabotaging behaviours, you will be better able to adopt more resourceful beliefs and behaviours.

Primal self-limiting belief	Common active compensatory behaviours	Common passive compensatory behaviours
"I AM UNWORTHY" *See list of remedial affirmations on page 102*	Being a perfectionist Boasting or being arrogant Seeking approval or attention Blaming or judging others Holding prejudice, including racism, sexism, classism, nationalism or ageism Obsessing with one's appearance or material, social, professional or academic status Being overly-concerned about other people's opinions of oneself Engaging in vandalism	Withdrawing from social interaction Not being assertive Being unmotivated Giving up too readily Being passive/aggressive Avoiding telling the truth Being overly-concerned about other people's opinions of oneself Sulking

Primal self-limiting belief	Common active compensatory behaviours	Common passive compensatory behaviours
"I AM UNSAFE" (Relating to physical, financial or time) *See list of remedial affirmations on page 106*	Needing to be in control Needing to always be in charge Over-planning Being unable to delegate Telling lies, cheating or stealing Attempting to manipulate or bully people Worrying obsessively about finances or the future Engaging in violence	Being unwilling to step out of one's comfort zone or participate in a new activity Resisting change Withholding information Avoiding particular modes of transport Worrying about finances or the future and doing nothing about it
"I AM ALONE" *See list of remedial affirmations on page 109*	Substance addictions (alcohol, nicotine, caffeine, prescription or illegal drugs or over-eating) Process addictions (workaholic, gym junkie, sex addict, computer games fanatic, television addict or other compulsive behaviours) Being unable to sit still or be silent Needing constant stimulation	Withdrawing from social interaction Being bored Being depressed Feeling unmotivated Lacking trust in others Losing faith in the future Losing belief in love

SECTION 4

CONSCIOUS DEFINITIONS OF TERMS

CONSCIOUS DEFINITIONS **OF TERMS**

> 66 *Michael and Robert's definitions of words and terms come from a diverse range of sources and experiences.* 99

Listed below are the authors' definitions of words and terms used throughout this book. They have come from a diverse range of sources and experiences that have influenced Michael and Robert's outlook.

Abundance consciousness
A belief that the universe is infinite and that all scarcity is fundamentally linked to limited thinking.

Acceptance
The state of allowing people and things to be the way they are, without the desire to change them.

Affirmation
A positive statement designed to improve the quality of your life.

Aggressor consciousness
The state of mind of a person who is reacting with force to circumstances or other people; the state of mind of a bully.

Anger
A reactive feeling, stemming from an attempt to re-empower oneself through an effort of force.

Anxiety
A mild form of fear.

Belief
A firmly held opinion; a thought accompanied by a feeling.

Closed-heartedness
A defensive state, which occurs when a person does not fully trust themselves and life.

Conditioned response
A learned response, which can be conscious or unconscious.

Connectedness
The feeling that occurs when you are open and empathetic towards others. Connection is our deepest desire.

Conscious mind
The thoughts and beliefs of which you are aware.

Creator consciousness
Your state of mind when your life is operating as you wish it to be.

Detachment
The state of being emotionally neutral; having a willingness to accept whatever is happening or not happening. This occurs when you believe that you are worthy, safe and connected.

Emotion
A reactive feeling, which is created by a chemical reaction taking place in your body. The three categories of reactive feelings are fear, anger and sadness.

Emotional responsibility
The ability to take charge of your emotions by remaining detached, open and accepting of yourself, others and life's circumstances at all times.

Empowerment
Your ability to discern the difference between resourceful and unresourceful thoughts and actions, and act accordingly.

Fear
A reactive feeling, stemming from a primal survival mechanism. It is often activated by past anxieties being projected into the future.

Feeling
A sensation in your body, which is a form of non-verbal communication.

Force
An act of wilfulness.

Forgiveness
The cessation of angry or resentful thoughts and feelings towards yourself or others, which has the benefit of liberating yourself.

Future
A forward projection in time from the present moment.

Gratitude
The quality of being thankful for what you have or are experiencing, or even for what you wish to have or experience.

Grief
A form of sadness.

Happiness
A natural feeling, in which you are free of stress.

Joy
A natural feeling, which is the consequence of having embraced love.

Love
A natural feeling, based on acceptance of yourself and others.

Natural feeling states
Feelings which are inherent to your true nature. They comprise love, joy and peace.

Open-heartedness
A state of being, which occurs when you fully trust yourself and life.

Pain
A feedback mechanism when one is out of touch with reality. Emotionally, pain is an unresolved feeling. Physically, pain is tension in the body, producing discomfort. If in place for too long, it will manifest as disease. Spiritually, pain is the experience of separation from oneself and others.

Past
A recollection in the present moment of an event that has occurred. All recollections are partial and subjective.

Peace
A natural feeling, free of mental chatter.

Personal growth
A process of increasing your personal power and capacity to love.

Personality
The conscious and unconscious memories and beliefs programmed into your mind and body.

Personal power
The state of being authentic, true to your principles and maintaining your integrity.

Personal responsibility
An attitude to life, where you understand and act upon the principle that you are the only one who can improve the quality of your life.

Positive belief
A resourceful belief that creates connection, abundance and unity.

Present time
This moment now; the only reality that exists.

Reactive feeling
An emotion activated from a conditioned response of the Personality.

Resourceful thoughts, beliefs and actions
Those that conserve and build energy, thus increasing the vitality of your body.

Sadness
A reactive feeling, based on a perceived loss.

Safe
The feeling that you are secure within yourself, which is not dependent upon others or life's circumstances.

Scarcity consciousness
A type of limited thinking, stemming from a belief that material, financial or human resources are limited.

Self-limiting belief
Any belief that is unresourceful, separates or discriminates against people, denies personal responsibility or is based upon scarcity.

Stress
An emotional and physical state that a person experiences when they fear that their desired outcome will differ from the actual one. This occurs when one believes that one is unworthy, unsafe and/or alone.

Thought
A concept or idea.

Trust
Faith in yourself, which you often project onto others and your life's circumstances.

Truth
A perspective that conserves and builds energy.

Unconscious mind
Thoughts and beliefs of which you are not fully aware, but which influence your actions and feelings. Often referred to as the "subconscious mind".

Victim consciousness
The state of mind of a person who believes that they are at the mercy of other people or external circumstances.

Wholeness
The state of being fully integrated with the physical, mental, emotional and spiritual components of yourself.

Worry
A reactive feeling and mental state, emanating from a lack of inner security.

Worthy
Self-accepting.

Zip-a-Dee-Doo-Dah
Not an actual word, but a light-hearted attitude to life!

SECTION 5

JOURNAL OF
SELF-DISCOVERY

JOURNAL OF
SELF-DISCOVERY

" *The affirmations for which you have the strongest reaction (either positive or negative) are the ones you may consider focusing upon.* "

This journal is to help you observe how your thoughts can change your feelings.

Simply describe with words or images how you feel before and after saying each day's affirmation in Section 2. Alternatively, you could use a scale from 1 to 10 where 1 to 5 is feeling bad and 6 to 10 is feeling good.

The affirmations for which you have the strongest reaction (either positive or negative) are the ones you may consider focusing upon. Enjoy your journal!

My feelings before saying today's affirmation	My feelings after saying today's affirmation
Day 1	

My feelings before saying today's affirmation	My feelings after saying today's affirmation
Day 2	
Day 3	
Day 4	
Day 5	

My feelings before saying today's affirmation	My feelings after saying today's affirmation
Day 6	
Day 7	
Day 8	
Day 9	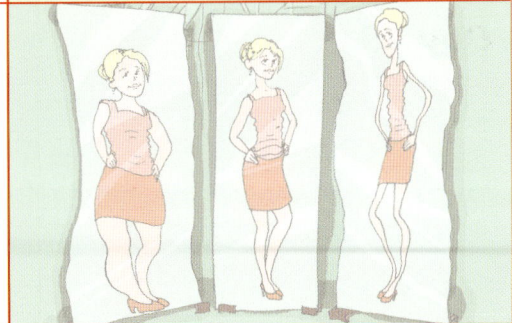

My feelings before saying today's affirmation	My feelings after saying today's affirmation
Day 10	
Day 11	
Day 12	
Day 13	

My feelings before saying today's affirmation	My feelings after saying today's affirmation
Day 14	
Day 15	
Day 16	
Day 17	

My feelings before saying today's affirmation	My feelings after saying today's affirmation
Day 18	
Day 19	
Day 20	
Day 21	

My feelings before saying today's affirmation	My feelings after saying today's affirmation
Day 22	
Day 23	
Day 24	
Day 25	

My feelings before saying today's affirmation	My feelings after saying today's affirmation
Day 26	
Day 27	
Day 28	
Day 29	

My feelings before saying today's affirmation	My feelings after saying today's affirmation
Day 30	
Day 31	

Our
*essential
nature is love.*

Our
*higher purpose
is to consciously
reconnect to our
essential nature
by giving and
receiving love.*

We
*are returning
to love.*

Connect with Say Hello To Happiness
on Facebook

PORPOISE
PRESS

WITH HEARTFELT **GRATITUDE**

Michael would like to express his gratitude to the following people for their love, friendship and support:

Susie Farrell, Serena Adamedes, Rahm Adamedes and Meleuka Morton- Masterman, John and Shizuyo Adamedes, Maria Adamedes, Peter and Karen Adamedes, Stacie and Liam Adamedes, Tom and Karen Anderson, Sue Barker, Denise Burgess, Ahrara Carisbrooke, Paul and Annie Davies, Lynne Gilkeson, Richard and Robyn Grzegrzulka, Peter and Jodie James, Catherine Lezer and Kevin McIsaac, Nigel and Deborah Lovell, Anitra Morgana, Robert Prior, Wayan and Yani Pughi, Satyananda Saraswati, Ahmid Sufi, Emmanuel Varipatis, Quentin Watts, Mark and Angela Williams.

Robert would like to express his gratitude to the following people for their love, friendship and support:

Michael Adamedes, Peter Astley, Michael Barg, Glenn Bidmead, Heiron Chan, Judith Collinge, William de Ora, Gillian Duguid, Sue Endres, David Faen, Keegan Fiertl, Murray and Jacky Gibbs, Angela Goussetis, Rob Gower, Alex Gruia, Ron and Monica Huban, Ian Langham, John Lofts, Elizabeth May, Pete Melov, Nicole Mohay, Vahini Naidoo, Peter and Jenny Norris-Smith, Ryan O'Loughlin, George Papanicolaou, Jane Prior and Geoff Eades, John Prior, Chris Short, Simon Thomson, Brad Tobias, Paul Williams, Ric Williams and Michael Wu.

Michael and Robert would like to express their gratitude to the following inspirational people: Justin Belitz, John Bradshaw, Deepak Chopra, Wayne Dyer, Ruth Fishel, Stanislav Grof, David Hawkins, Louise Hay, Arthur Janov, Susan Jeffers, Ken Keyes, Robert Kiyosaki, Joseph Murphy, Leonard Orr, Osho, M. Scott Peck, Sondra Ray, Richard Sutphen, Eckhart Tolle and Loy Young.

Special thanks to Tetiana Koldunenko for her wonderful artwork, Veacha Sen for her uplifting layout, Murray Gibbs for his insightful editorial support, and Zoran Zocoski for his creative cover design.

Our heartfelt thanks also to all the wonderful people, too numerous to mention, who have shared their time and love on our extraordinary journey of discovery.

Finally, we thank you, dear reader, for aspiring to improve yourself and make this world a better place.

ش dank u Շնորհակալություն təşəkkür edirəm eskerrik asko merci
якуй তোমাকে ধন্যবাদ благодаря gràcies 谢谢 hvala děkuji хва
kuji tak dank u aitäh salamat kiitos merci grazas მადლობა dz
ლობა danke σας ευχαριστώ આભાર di ou mèsi תודה शुक्रिया mult
szönöm शुक्रिया þakka þér terima kasih buíochas a ghabháil leat
íochas a ghabháil leat grazie ありがとう gratias agimus tibi спаси
ㅺㅼㅽㅾㄿ paldies ačiū 감사합니다 ви благодариме terima kasih
rima kasih nirringrazzjak takk dziękuję مشکرازرکشتاب obrigado
ulţumesc спасибо хвала ďakujem hvala gracias asante takk d
ck நன்றி спасибі дякую ధన్యవాదాలు teşekkür ederim mulţum
 บคุณ cảm ơn bạn diolch yn fawr thank you děkuji tak dank u dzi
ank you спасибо merci dankie ju falenderoj σας ευχαριστώ хва
ش dank u Շնորհակալություն təşəkkür edirəm eskerrik asko danki
якуй তোমাকে ধন্যবাদ благодаря gràcies 谢谢 hvala děkuji mul
kuji tak dank u aitäh salamat kiitos merci grazas მადლობა da
ლობა शुक्रिया danke σας ευχαριστώ આભાર di ou mèsi תודה thank
szönöm terima kasih शुक्रिया buíochas a ghabháil leat təşəkkür ed
íochas a ghabháil leat grazie ありがとう agimus tibi gratias þakk
ㅺㅼㅽㅾㄿ paldies ačiū 감사합니다 ви благодариме terima kasih
rima kasih nirringrazzjak takk dziękuję مشکرازرکشتاب obrigado
ulţumesc спасибо хвала ďakujem hvala gracias asante takk th
ck நன்றி спасибі дякую ధన్యవాదాలు teşekkür ederim дякую
บคุณ cảm ơn bạn diolch yn fawr thank you děkuji tak dank u ait
ank you спасибо merci dankie ju falenderoj σας ευχαριστώ dan
ش dank u Շնորհակալություն təşəkkür edirəm eskerrik asko ви бл
якуй তোমাকে ধন্যবাদ благодаря gràcies 谢谢 hvala děkuji þak
kuji tak dank u aitäh salamat kiitos merci grazas მადლობა da
ლობა danke σας ευχαριστώ આભાર di ou mèsi תודה शुक्रिया спас
szönöm शुक्रिया þakka þér terima kasih buíochas a ghabháil leat
íochas a ghabháil leat grazie ありがとう gratias agimus tibi esker
ㅺㅼㅽㅾㄿ paldies ačiū 감사합니다 ви благодариме terima kasih
rima kasih nirringrazzjak takk dziękuję مشکرازرکشتاب obrigado
ulţumesc спасибо хвала ďakujem hvala gracias asante takk σ
ck நன்றி спасибі дякую ధన్యవాదాలు teşekkür ederim дякую
บคุณ cảm ơn bạn diolch yn fawr thank you děkuji tak dank u dz
kuji tak dank u aitäh salamat kiitos merci grazas მადლობა ta
ლობა danke σας ευχαριστώ આભાર di ou mèsi תודה शुक्रिया than
ش dank u Շնորհակալություն təşəkkür edirəm eskerrik asko obrig